# Spring Rose, Winter Bear

by Dale Cooper
illustrated by Sheila Bailey

PEARSON

Scott
Foresman

Editorial Offices: Glenview, Illinois • Parsippany, New Jersey • New York, New York
Sales Offices: Needham, Massachusetts • Duluth, Georgia • Glenview, Illinois
Coppell, Texas • Sacramento, California • Mesa, Arizona

Seasons come and go.
People change their ways.

Animals and plants change too.
Let's find out how.

In the fall, a bear eats and eats.
The bear needs fat before it snows.
The bear sleeps all winter in its
warm den.

In the spring, the bear wakes up.
Oh, good-bye, den!
That's right. It's time to eat again.

In the winter, this fox's coat gets white.
It looks just like the snow.

In the summer, its fur gets brown.
It looks just like the ground.

winter

summer

In the winter, how does this bird change?
It grows bumps on the edges of its feet!
Then it won't sink in the deepest snow.

winter

In the winter, the hedge has no roses.

It gets warmer in the spring.
Then roses grow on the hedge.

winter

spring

In the spring, an apple tree grows white flowers.

In the summer and fall, its apples grow. They can be red, green, or yellow.

spring

fall

Trees need the summer sun.
It helps their leaves get green.

In the fall, the days get shorter.
The leaves turn colors and fall off.

In the winter, most trees are bare.

But in the spring, their leaves grow back. Soon the leaves will be green again.

Seasons come and go.
People change their ways.
Animals and plants change too.
Do you remember how?